Shells on their Backs

Written by Anna Porter
Series Consultant: Linda Hoyt

WorldWise
Content-based Learning

Contents

Introduction

Imagine carrying a heavy backpack that weighs as much as two elephants! That's a lot like what many turtles and tortoises have to do. All turtles and tortoises have a shell on their back, and for some, this shell can weigh 200 times more than their own body weight!

These amazing, ancient reptiles have lived on Earth for over 200 million years. This means they lived on this planet even before the dinosaurs. They have survived longer than most other animals on Earth. Today, turtles and tortoises are still found all over the world.

But many species are at risk of survival in our modern world.

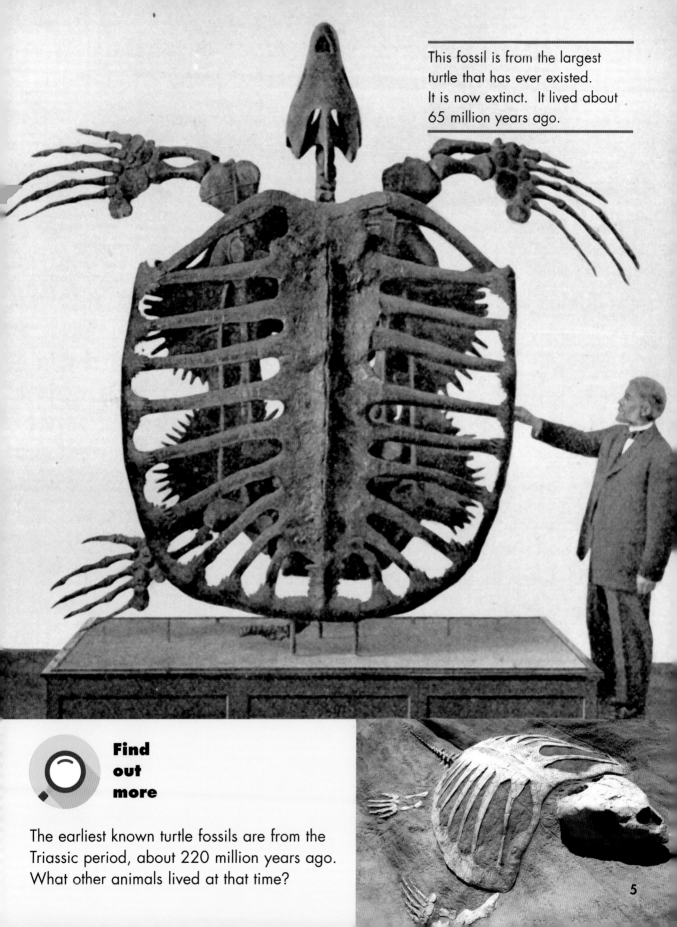

This fossil is from the largest turtle that has ever existed. It is now extinct. It lived about 65 million years ago.

Find out more

The earliest known turtle fossils are from the Triassic period, about 220 million years ago. What other animals lived at that time?

Chapter 1

Shells on their backs

Find out more

Turtles and tortoises are reptiles. Can you name some other reptiles?

Turtles and tortoises are reptiles. Like all reptiles, they have a backbone and scaly skin, and they are cold-blooded. This means that their body temperature is the same as the water or air that surrounds them.

What makes turtles and tortoises different from all other reptiles is that they have a large shell on their back.

		Habitat	Food
Turtles	**Sea turtles**	Aquatic – Seawater mostly, lay eggs on land	**Carnivores:** some species eat sea creatures **Herbivores:** some species eat sea grasses **Omnivores:** some species eat both sea grasses and sea creatures
	Freshwater turtles	Aquatic – Fresh water mainly, some time on land	**Omnivores:** small fish, insects and vegetation
	Terrapins	Semi-aquatic – Mix of fresh water and salt water, lay eggs on land	**Omnivores:** small invertebrates, sea vegetation
Tortoises		Land	**Herbivores:** cacti, grasses, fruit and other vegetation

▲ Leopard tortoise

Turtles and tortoises - what's the difference?

There are many differences between turtles and tortoises. These include their size, the shape and hardness of their shells, their beaks, their feet and legs, and what they need to survive.

But the main difference is where they spend most of their time. Turtles live in water, either seawater or fresh water. Tortoises live on land.

◀ Green sea turtle

Beak	Shell shape	Feet
Shape is adapted to the type of food each species eats	Streamlined for swimming	Flippers, with one or two claws on the front flippers
Powerful jaws and a hooked beak	Streamlined for swimming	Webbed feet and long claws
Strong jaws for crushing shells	Streamlined for swimming	Webbed feet and long claws
Short beak for chewing tough plants in dry places	High domed shell	Short stumpy legs, sturdy flat feet with claws

The shell

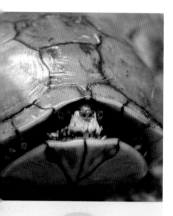

Turtles and tortoises all have shells that cover most of their body. These shells vary in colour, shape and size. Most shells are hard and are like armour that protects these reptiles from predators. When threatened, most turtles and tortoises can draw their heads and limbs back into their shells.

Sea turtles cannot pull their heads or limbs into their shells. Instead, they swim away from danger and close their tough eyelids to protect their eyes from attack.

Young turtles and tortoises have soft shells, and are most at risk from predators. As they grow, their shells harden.

Did you know?

The bone plates on the top of the shell are made of scales called **scutes**. These are made from **keratin**, like our fingernails or the hooves of some animals.

carapace

bone plates on the top of the carapace are called scutes

bone plates in the underlayer of the carapace join to the backbone and ribs

bony bridge joins the top and bottom of the shell

plastron

A long life span

Turtles and tortoises live longer than most other animals. Larger species can live from 80 years to almost 200 years, and smaller species can live for about 40 years. No one is sure why they have such long life spans. Some scientists think it's because their bodies convert the food they eat into energy very slowly. Also, because they move very slowly, they don't use much energy.

Breeding

These reptiles do not begin breeding until they are at least seven years old, and some do not start until they are 20 years old.

Female turtles and tortoises dig a nest in sand or mud to lay their eggs. They then leave their nest and their eggs. Most turtles and tortoises lay a large number of eggs to give their young the best chance of surviving. None of them look after their young.

The temperature of the nest affects the eggs as they **incubate**. In warmer nests, more hatchlings are female. In cooler nests, more hatchlings are male.

▲ This tortoise is laying her eggs in a burrow that she has dug in mud.

◀ A green sea turtle digs a burrow in the sand in which to lay her eggs.

Chapter 2

Turtles

Turtles live most of their lives in or around either seawater or fresh water. They have developed a body shape that allows them to swim easily. Some turtles have webbed feet, and others have flippers. They cannot breathe under water and come to the surface for air every few minutes when they are swimming. But many can stay under water and hold their breath for quite some time when they are resting.

▼ Green sea turtle

Find out more

What is the largest sea turtle species? How much does it weigh? Find out more about its shell. What is the smallest sea turtle, and how much does it weigh?

Sea turtles

The ancestors of sea turtles lived on land. Over time, they spent more and more time in the water. Today, they are found in all warm-water areas of the world.

Sea turtles hunt for food such as crabs, clams and sea plants. This gives them the energy to travel the long distances between their feeding and nesting areas.

Nesting

Once a year, female sea turtles return to the beaches where they were born to lay their eggs. They come ashore at night and use the moonlight to find their way up the sandy beaches. It is difficult for the turtles to move on the sand with their flippers. They dig a nest with their flippers and lay their eggs in it.

After laying the eggs, the female uses her flippers to cover them with sand and then returns to the sea. After about 60 days, the young turtles hatch. They wait for nightfall before scrambling over the sand to the sea, where they begin swimming.

▼ Newly hatched Olive Ridley turtles make their way to the ocean.

Find out more

Young green sea turtles are **omnivores,** but when they reach adulthood they change to **herbivores.** Find out how their diet changes. What do they eat when they are young? What do they eat when they become adults?

Freshwater turtles

Freshwater turtles live in wetlands, swamps, rivers and lakes. They come in many sizes, shapes and colours and most are smaller than sea turtles.

These turtles do not have flippers. They have webbing between their toes to help them swim. Sometimes they come out of the water and climb onto logs or rocks to lie in the sun for a short time to warm up their bodies.

Most freshwater turtles are active during the day, looking for food under water. They eat insects, fish and some plants. They use their strong jaws to get their food and to protect themselves.

Find out more

Terrapins are a type of freshwater turtle that lives in coastal swamps and marshes that are flooded by the sea at high tide. Their habitat is a mixture of salt water and fresh water.

These reptiles drink fresh water to survive. They take in a lot of salt because they catch their food in the water. How do they get rid of this excess salt? What else can you find out about terrapins?

These turtles are sitting on a log in a pond, basking in the sun.

▲ This large freshwater turtle is called a snapping turtle. It has laid its eggs in a burrow in the ground, which it will cover with dirt.

Each year, these turtles come out of the water to lay their eggs in the sand or the mud. The young hatch after 45 days in warmer places and 90 days in cooler places.

In winter, freshwater turtles that live in cooler climates burrow into mud or sand at the bottom of the water and hibernate. They rest for up to three months without eating and use very little oxygen from the water.

Find out more

What is the largest freshwater turtle in Australia? Where does it live and what does it eat?

13

Chapter 3

Tortoises

Tortoises live on land, often in places that are very dry.

Tortoises get some water from the plants that they eat. They can live without fresh water for a year. When it rains, they dig a hole to collect fresh water. They store the water they drink in their bladders and draw upon this supply when needed.

Unlike turtles, tortoises do not have webbed feet, and they cannot swim. Their feet are hard and stumpy for walking on land and across sharp rocks.

▼ Tortoises can live in dry places. They get water from the plants they eat.

Did you know?

In Ancient Roman warfare, soldiers held their shields tightly together in front of or above them, to create a tight formation. They called this a testudo formation. *Testudo* is the Latin word for tortoise.

Burrows

Tortoises dig burrows that they use for shelter from the hot sun and to rest. Resting in burrows helps them lower their body temperature. It also reduces the amount of water they lose from their bodies through **evaporation**. Tortoises use a burrow for a few days before moving on to find more food and dig another burrow.

When they are ready to breed, tortoises lay their eggs in nests close to their burrows.

Tortoises move very slowly, so they use little energy. They move about and feed during spring, summer and autumn. In winter, they dig another burrow and hibernate. This helps them survive cold winters.

◀ A Western Hermann's tortoise hibernating in the ground

Find out more

What other animals make use of the burrows dug by tortoises?

15

Desert tortoises

The desert tortoise can live in areas where the temperature may exceed 60 degrees Celsius. It digs a burrow up to two metres deep to escape the heat. This helps it avoid losing water from its body through evaporation. These burrows also allow it to survive the colder winter months.

Desert tortoises get most of the water they need from the plants they eat, even during the hottest, driest times of the year.

When threatened by a predator, the tortoise can withdraw its head and legs into its shell. Adult tortoises are rarely preyed upon, but animals such as foxes, badgers, ravens and coyotes often dig up their eggs and hunt hatchlings. Desert tortoises can live for up to 50 years in the wild.

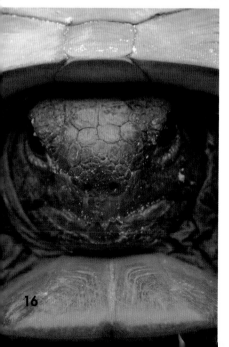

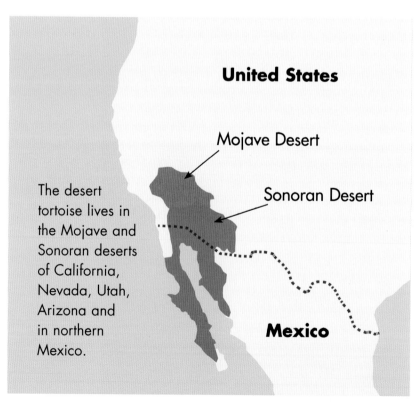

United States

Mojave Desert

Sonoran Desert

The desert tortoise lives in the Mojave and Sonoran deserts of California, Nevada, Utah, Arizona and in northern Mexico.

Mexico

Threats to desert tortoises

The survival of some desert tortoises is threatened. Their habitat is being destroyed so that houses, farms and factories can be built. Roads have also been made through their **foraging** areas. When the desert tortoises wander onto the roads, they are likely to be crushed.

People have also introduced new plant species such as buffel grass and red brome that crowded out the plants that desert tortoises eat. Viruses and diseases also pose a risk. The decline in desert tortoise numbers is most severe in the western Mojave Desert.

Protecting desert tortoises

In California, the Desert Tortoise Preserve Committee protects about 2,000 hectares of desert tortoise habitat. It is now unlawful to touch or collect wild desert tortoises. Despite the laws that protect them, their numbers are still declining.

▼ When desert tortoises wander onto roads, they can be run over by cars and killed.

Giant tortoises

The giant tortoise is best known for its size and for how long it lives. These reptiles used to live throughout the world. Many have become extinct, and today only two species survive – the Galápagos tortoise and the Aldabra tortoise. They live on remote islands, where there are few natural predators, and can live for more than 100 years.

Galápagos tortoises

North America

Atlantic Ocean

Pacific Ocean

Galápagos Islands

South America

	Galápagos tortoise	**Aldabra tortoise**
Size	Average length: 1.5 metres Average weight: 250 kilograms	Average length: 1.2 metres Average weight: 250 kilograms
Numbers in the wild	19,000	100,000
Status	Vulnerable to extinction	Vulnerable to extinction

Aldabra tortoises

Europe

Asia

Pacific Ocean

Africa

Aldabra Islands

Indian Ocean

Australia

Southern Ocean

Galápagos giant tortoise

The Galápagos giant tortoise lives only in the hot and dry conditions of the Galápagos Islands. It is the largest living tortoise, and if it could stand up it would be 1.5 metres tall. It eats cactus plants, leaves and fruit that grow naturally on the islands. The Galápagos giant tortoise starts breeding when it is about 40 years of age.

The Galápagos giant tortoise was discovered almost 500 years ago by Spanish explorers. The Spanish word for tortoise is *galápago*. Scientists estimate the population of tortoises at that time was about 250,000. By 1974, only about 3,000 were left. The numbers dropped because thousands were taken from the islands, they were eaten by people visiting or living there, or the tortoises' natural food source was destroyed when people introduced animals and cleared the land to grow crops.

Think about ...

The Galápagos giant tortoise is a protected animal, and the islands where they live form a World Heritage Conservation Area. What might this mean for people wanting to visit these islands?

Bartolome Island, Galápagos Islands, Ecuador

When people realised that the number of tortoises was dangerously low, they started to protect the tortoises' nests. They collected the eggs and took them to the Charles Darwin Research Station on one of the islands so that young tortoises could hatch in a protected area.

Since this program began, over 2,000 tortoises have been safely returned to their island homes. Today, there are about 19,000 Galápagos giant tortoises.

◀ Baby Galápagos tortoises

 Find out more
Who was Charles Darwin, and what did he study on the Galápagos Islands?

An Aldabra giant tortoise

Find out more

Where can the Aldabra giant tortoise be found in zoos around the world?

The Aldabra giant tortoise

The Aldabra giant tortoise is found only on the Aldabra Islands, in the Seychelles in the Indian Ocean. These islands are part of a coral reef **atoll** and people do not live there. About 100,000 giant tortoises live in the scrub, swamps or grassy plains of these islands.

This giant tortoise eats grasses, leaves and the stems of plants. It gets the water it needs from its food, as there is very little fresh water on these islands.

This island in the Seychelles is now a bio-reserve and home to more than 300 Aldabra giant tortoises.

These tortoises do not start breeding until they are around 25–30 years old. They breed once or twice a year, and the female lays about 25 eggs in a dry, shallow nest in the ground. The eggs and hatchlings do not have a high rate of survival.

The Aldabra giant tortoise is one of the longest-living animals on Earth. One tortoise is over 170 years old and is thought to be the oldest living giant tortoise.

This animal's **conservation** level in the world is listed as vulnerable or could become extinct. Today, the whole atoll is a protected World Heritage Conservation Area. Some Aldabra tortoises are kept in conservation parks on other islands in the Indian Ocean or in zoos, to try to protect them from extinction.

23

Chapter 4

Protecting turtles and tortoises

Although turtles and tortoises can live a long time, many are listed as endangered because of hunting and habitat loss.

Hunting

People still hunt turtles and tortoises and use them for food, in traditional medicines, or sell them as pets. Some are killed for their meat and so that products from their shells can be made and sold. Sea turtles can get caught in fishing nets and drown, or become trapped under crab and lobster traps.

This loggerhead sea turtle is entangled with garbage. Turtles can die when they get entangled with garbage or nets. This one was rescued.

Habitat loss

Over time, people have used more and more land for agriculture, housing and industry. They have also cleared land to build roads. This has led to the destruction of the habitats where many land-based turtles and tortoises breed.

People are working to protect the habitats where these reptiles live and to make sure that there is enough food for them. Some coastal areas are now listed as Marine Protected Areas. Fishing is restricted in these areas so that sea turtles are not caught on lines or in nets.

Think about ...

Turtles and tortoises are easy to keep as pets. Many of the 23 threatened species of turtle and tortoise can be found for sale online. Why can this business be dangerous to their survival?

A small fence keeps endangered desert tortoises from wandering onto the highway. Tortoise populations in the western Mojave Desert have dropped nearly 90 per cent in the past three decades.

Global warming

Scientists predict that increasing global temperatures will affect all stages of the lives of turtles and tortoises. Warmer temperatures are causing sea levels to rise and destroy beaches. Some of these beaches are nesting sites for sea turtles.

As temperatures rise, the sand on beaches where sea turtles build nests becomes warmer. When the nest conditions become warmer, it is more likely that the young will be female. Scientists predict that if there are far more female turtles than males, it could affect their ability to reproduce and lay eggs.

Warmer sea temperatures will also cause marine plants to die, so there will be less food for the plant-eating sea turtles. These changes may lead to the extinction of many species.

This beach in Costa Rica is an important nesting site for sea turtles, including the endangered green sea turtle. Rising sea levels could destroy this beach.

Using technology to study turtles and tortoises

Technology is helping scientists monitor turtles and tortoises and to learn about their behaviour. Some threatened species have been fitted with a **GPS** "backpack" that helps scientists track their movements and protect nesting sites. Other reptiles have a small **microchip** inserted into their shoulder muscles. This provides information about when eggs are laid and how many **clutches** are laid in a season.

Scientists also use electronic devices to record nest temperatures during the time that eggs are **incubating**. They do this to learn about the way temperature changes affect whether the hatchlings are male or female.

Wildlife **conservation** organisations, such as the World Wide Fund for Nature, work with local communities to monitor and protect the nesting sites of turtles and tortoises.

▲ A Kemp's Ridley sea turtle with a tracking device on its back.

▲ A scientist records the temperature of a nesting site.

▲ A park ranger monitors and documents a Kemp's Ridley sea turtle laying a clutch of eggs.

Mapping sea turtles' nesting sites

Think about ...

Why do you think the transmitter tags send signals only when the turtle comes to the water's surface?

Scientists are concerned about threats to sea turtles and want to find out more about their behaviour so they can help protect them. To do this, they capture sea turtles at sea, attach an electronic tag to each turtle's shell so it can be monitored by satellite, and release the turtles back into the sea.

When the turtle is under the water, the tag switches off, so its location is not known. But when the turtle comes to the surface to breathe, the tag switches on and sends a signal of its location to a satellite in space. This signal identifies its location.

A young loggerhead turtle with a tracking device attached to its shell.

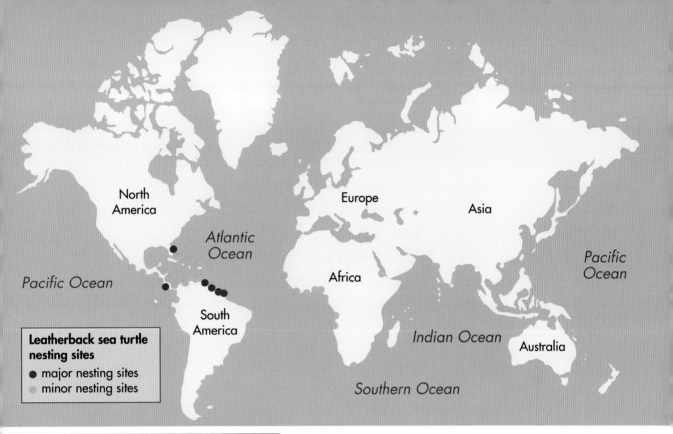

Leatherback sea turtle nesting sites
- major nesting sites
- minor nesting sites

North America
Atlantic Ocean
Pacific Ocean
South America
Europe
Asia
Africa
Pacific Ocean
Indian Ocean
Australia
Southern Ocean

Scientists then log each location on a map. Using this information, scientists can map nesting areas around the world and try to have these places protected.

When female sea turtles nest, they come ashore to lay their eggs at night. After hatching, the young make their way to the sea at night. Adults and young are guided to the sea by landmarks and moonlight. But the lights from cars and buildings can confuse them, and they can go in the wrong direction. They dry out and die, or are attacked by predators. Scientists know that this is happening because of the satellite images from the tags, and they want lights near these beaches turned off late at night to protect the sea turtles.

29

Conclusion

Many species of turtles and tortoises are threatened with extinction. Human activities such as commercial fishing, habitat destruction, and climate change have contributed to this situation. We need to act now so that their numbers can be replenished. Laws have been passed to protect some nesting sites. Scientists have set up special breeding areas. **Conservation** groups and volunteers work to monitor turtle and tortoise numbers and keep their nesting areas clean.

You can help, too. Try to remember:

- Keep beaches clear of rubbish. Remember to take plastic bags away from the beach so that they don't get washed out to sea and choke turtles.

- Be careful not to disturb nesting female turtles. Always obey the signs about areas to avoid.

- Turn off car headlights if you go to a turtle-nesting beach at night. Artificial light can distract a female sea turtle or the new hatchlings from following their natural path back to the sea.

- Do not buy products made from turtles or tortoises.

Glossary

atoll an island made of coral

carnivores animals that eat meat

clutches groups of eggs

conservation to protect something and keep it in its natural environment

evaporation changing from liquid into vapour

foraging searching for food

GPS a navigation system that uses satellite signals

herbivores animals that eat plants

incubate to help eggs hatch by keeping them warm

keratin the material that hair and nails are made from; feathers, horns and claws are also made from keratin

microchip a very small computer chip that stores information

omnivores animals that eat plants and animals

scutes thick, bony plates on a turtle or tortoise's shell

Index